Anger Management

Get To Know Your Triggers, Master The Art Of Self-control, And Build A Positive Bond With Your Child

(A Must-Have Manual For Building Emotional Resilience, Recognising And Avoiding Triggers, And Raising Children With Love, Discipline, And Self-Assurance)

AngioloCampanella

TABLE OF CONTENT

Is Stress A Bad Thing Overall?.....................1

Rage's Symptoms And Indicators, Including Persistent Rage........................... 18

How Does Anger Affect You?..................... 44

Manage Your Anger Before It Takes Over You 94

Impact Of Anger... 115

Is Stress A Bad Thing Overall?

While not entirely negative, stress played a crucial role in our survival, just as it did for our hunter-gatherer predecessors. Utilizing the trigger to avoid potentially fatal scenarios or maintain composure in a tumultuous setting could be helpful.

People view stress differently; for some, it may be a natural part of daily life.

Take public speaking, for example. While some people enjoy the surge of adrenaline, others find the thought of it numbs them.

Although stress is generally seen negatively, there are situations in which it can be beneficial—if you only feel it for a short period. Once you've passed the agitated stage—also referred to as the fight-or-flight response—you should return to yourself.

Your body should return to its previous state with no lasting effects in a short period. Therefore, chronic stress is always a contributing factor to several health concerns if left unchecked.

According to research, 80% of Americans said they had seen at least one sign of stress the month before. Twenty percent or so reported feeling pressured. Living a stress-free existence is difficult due to the nature of life. On the other hand, we can learn how to manage it when we can't avoid it when necessary.

Stress types

There are three main categories of stress:

Acute episodes of stress (EAS)

severe stress

prolonged or persistent stress

Acute strain

Most people experience acute stress at some time. This happens to be the body's first response to unfamiliar activities. It's the anxiousness that can arise from almost avoiding a car crash. Acute stress might happen, for instance, while you're sliding down a steep mountain slope or experiencing an emotional rollercoaster.

These episodes of extreme stress typically don't hurt you. Thus, it could benefit you for a few reasons. Stress makes your body and brain better handle challenging situations later on. After the threat is eliminated, your biological processes should remain unchanged.

In the event of very acute stress, a DIFFERENT STORY is told. Stresses like these can cause complex problems like PTSD and other mental health concerns when they are experienced in complex scenarios.

Periodic severe stress

It is the outcome of ongoing, severe stress. If you have frequent anxiety and worry about potential events, it might grow.

You can feel as though your life is in disarray and that you are always experiencing tragedies. Certain professions, like law enforcement or firefighting, could also frequently expose you to stressful situations. Regular occurrences of extreme acute stress can be detrimental to one's physical and mental well-being.

persistent stress

The main cause of chronic stress is excessive levels of stress experienced. Such chronic stress can be harmful to your health and increase your risk of developing conditions such as:

Uncertainty

inadequatedefenses

elevated blood pressure

Heart-related conditions

Depression

Prolonged stress can also be a factor in common symptoms like headaches, stomach troubles, and insomnia.

Thus, being aware of most stressors and how to manage them will benefit you.

sources of tension

going through a calamity, whether man-made or natural

having a persistent medical condition

escaping a disease or disaster that could kill you

becoming the victim of criminal activity, coping with difficulties in the family, like an abusive relationship

a miserable union

Previous Experiences

Sometimes, the things that have happened to you in the past could be the source of your anger. You might still be harboring anger without realizing it if you have previously been in situations that made you angry. Still, you had to control your anger at the time because there was nowhere to express it securely.

A person may become permanently enraged due to a variety of terrible situations, including trauma, abuse, and bullying. Studies have indicated that those who harass others typically experience bullying themselves.

If you are an employer and you bully your employees, it may be because you were bullied as a child or during your time in college or high school. Most people who bully others on social media are those who, in real life, are the targets of bullying.

Individuals who have previously experienced physical, verbal, emotional, or sexual abuse may become irate because of the pain they still carry from the abuse. A person may exhibit exceptional levels of aggression and anger against all members of the opposing sex if someone of the opposite sex sexually molested them.

Another event that could be the source of rage is trauma. The effects frequently last a lifetime even when a person believes they have gotten past a traumatic event. Anger episodes can be triggered by memories of prior trauma, which can also cause feelings of irritation, anxiety, and hopelessness.

Due to your past experiences, you are prone to irritation because certain situations are exceptionally difficult. There are situations when your anger is not a result of the circumstances you are in right now. Instead, they are connected to earlier encounters. This implies that anything from your past is reflected in the circumstances you find yourself in right now.

To address anger, you must first recognize the specific previous experience that is acting as the root cause of your anger.

Current Situation

There are instances in which the situation you're in right now is what makes you angry. You might discover that you are more prone to rage than ever if you have a lot going on. You can also be experiencing anger about completely unrelated issues.

Many people experience anger easily because they are in an enraged scenario, but they lack the confidence to confront or immediately handle the matter.

Let's examine an illustration. You will become enraged if your supervisor acts especially hostile or harshly towards you at work. You might not be brave enough to confront him about it, though, given that he is your boss.

This implies that you will need to contain your rage. However, the problem with rage is that it is short-lived. As a result, you might vent your rage on your family members or coworkers at work. Anger might be sparked by something as little as your toddler spilling water on the floor.

In this instance, your work environment is the source of your ire, but you don't feel equipped to confront it since you fear losing your job. This causes you to direct your rage at your coworkers or your impoverished children at home.

Being Powerless or Helpless

Anger is frequently sparked by this, especially among men. You can feel more sore than normal because you feel powerless and have no control over the issue. In this case, your boss at work is an example.

Feelings of helplessness and a loss of control over one's life's circumstances are frequently linked to powerlessness. People become enraged when circumstances beyond their control arise because they prefer to feel controlled.

You might experience extreme anger due to your perceived helplessness in situations where you are unable to escape, such as health problems or an abusive relationship.

Reminding yourself that some things will be within or outside your control is crucial in this situation. However, there are circumstances in which you have total control; all that is required of you is to use that control.

Anxiety and Stress

More than 40 million American adults—or about 18% of the country's total population—struggle with anxiety, according to figures released by the Anxiety and Depression Association.

Anger, stress, and anxiety are three closely related illnesses, as I have already explained. Overwhelming and uncontrollable reactions are common in people with anxiety-related disorders. They eventually resort to using rage to express their stress and dissatisfaction.

Because of the strain that stressful and unclear circumstances place on the shoulder and brain, they frequently cause people to get furious.

Sadness

Grief is the final frequent reason for rage that you should be aware of. Grief is usually an intense emotion that results from traumatic events. It is also connected to adversity and grief.

Grief can be experienced when a friend, pet, or loved one passes away. Professional and career-related events, such as losing your job, might also trigger it.

When grief takes hold of you, it can quickly turn into fury. This rage frequently results from the bereaved person feeling frustrated and unfairly treated. For example, if you lose your spouse, you may feel aggrieved, dissatisfied, and upset at the harshness and unfairness of your circumstances merely by remembering the future you both imagined.

You can be particularly angry at individuals for being unable to relate to you or feeling empathy for your predicament and suffering.

Other than the ones we just looked at together, several other factors could make you angry, even though you're unaware.

Rage's Symptoms And Indicators, Including Persistent Rage

All feel anger. A common human feeling spurs someone to action after an insult, attack, or violation. Our bodies' innate defense system allows us to defend ourselves, voice our opinions, and confront injustice. The body raises its noradrenaline, hormones, and adrenaline levels when irritated. Our bodies are pumped full of these potent compounds, giving us the strength and stamina to take on any perceived threat. Even though a hormone rush can somewhat disrupt our emotions when combined with two potent natural stimulants, your body and mind are poised to defend themselves. That's why, when the body goes into fight-or-flight mode, the natural way for someone to vent their rage is typically through aggressive behavior.

There is a distinction between occasionally losing your temper and becoming unable to manage your rage. There are a few crucial signs that could help determine whether you or a loved one is struggling with anger control.

Easily Angry

Everybody has moments when they get irascible. This is particularly true if you have a stressful life or are experiencing an emotionally taxing situation. It is your body's method of alerting you to the possibility of a chasm that could result in a breakdown. In situations like this, you usually find that your anger evens out, and you return to normal as soon as the strain and stress are released. The issue arises when you start losing your temper frequently and notice that your ability to tolerate rage seems to erode with each outburst. You have the impression that you are always unhappy and become enraged over seemingly insignificant things.

Not Able to Keep Up a Good Relationship

Anger may take many forms in a relationship, and no matter how much you love someone, there is only so much abuse a person can endure. Anger can manifest as a fear of communicating one's emotions in a relationship, resulting in inadequacy, distrust, or extreme shyness. Fear is one of the most volatile rage accelerants when managing a relationship. It can also cause someone to react in the most repulsive ways, including mistrust, jealousy, and verbal or physical violence. When rage festers inside a relationship and is uncontrolled, it usually leaves hurt and devastation. Unchecked anger management issues make it impossible for anyone to have a good relationship with anyone in their life.

Self-harm as a way to release frustration or rage

Venting your rage by hitting a wall or driving your nails into your hands is not a healthy coping strategy, nor does it indicate that you have regained control. Not only can it result in more lethal consequences, infections, or severe injuries, but it can also be a sign of more serious mental health problems. Low self-esteem, eating disorders, depression, anxiety, bipolar disease, and substance addiction are just a few conditions that can manifest as anger. It might also indicate maltreatment, sadness, or a past event you never fully moved behind or that you hold self-responsibility for.

Exuberant Conduct During Debates

Individuals who argue frequently, lose their cool easily, fight verbally or physically, or feel the need to toss objects may be experiencing explosive behavior. An individual with intermittent explosive disorder (IED) experiences sudden, violent outbursts that end almost as quickly as they started. When a little offense escalates into a significant one, it may appear they are completely overreacting to a situation and lack impulse control. After each outburst, they will display regret, guilt, and embarrassment over their actions. The majority of individuals with IEDs typically have an underlying illness, may have experienced a brain injury, or may run in the family.

Issues With Believing Others

Many people find it difficult to trust, particularly those struggling to control their anger. Jealousy is frequently the source of wrath, and jealousy can exacerbate someone's paranoia and foster mistrust. People who struggle with anger management typically believe that they cannot trust anyone, even those closest to them. They may even start stalking the person they don't trust. They might become very controlling, doubt everything, get fixated, and stop believing what they are told. Their demand for validation that their suspicions are well-founded stems from their urge to assign responsibility for the intense rage that motivates them. It is often simpler to call someone out for lying or cheating than to acknowledge that there might be an issue on their end.

Blackouts of rage

When someone becomes so enraged that they lose consciousness, this is known as a "rage blackout." They then go on the rampage, destroying everything and everyone in their path. They have amnesia and are detached when they do nearly superhuman accomplishments during the blackout. These blackouts often only last a few seconds to a few minutes, but they can potentially do significant harm during that time. Driven by the body's neurological system and neurotransmitters, they can accomplish things that, if not so horrifying, would be astounding. Some refer to it as "going berserk," a term originating from the Norse Berserker, who was thought to achieve a state in which they would have nearly superhuman power. Because of this, they could advance in combat and kill everything in their path. Their side would stay well out of their way or as far behind them as possible, foaming at the mouth and displaying bursts of extreme wrath, for the Berker could not tell a friend from an enemy. Until they regain consciousness, people who experience anger blackouts are powerless and forget what they did to cause the destruction. An excellent illustration of a disassociated anger blackout condition is The Incredible Hulk. Neither does Dr. Banner have any memory of what the Hulk does, nor is his entire existence changed into a strong, destructive monster over whom he has no control when he feels threatened or under pressure.

Abrupt Decline

Anger is a potent tool that can help someone feel in control of what they consider to be a threat again. When someone steps up to defend something or someone, it can occasionally be viewed as a heroic deed. Additionally, it can be used to mask emotions like worry, anxiety, and terror, giving the user the impression that they are back in control of the circumstance. Even when someone is fully aware of what they are doing, they cannot stop themselves because their anger fuels the underlying problems that cause them to lash out in a rage. Someone who has lost control of their anger is even more frightening than a fury blackout. Because they frequently zero in on their target with lethal accuracy while fully conscious of the damage they are causing.

Discover your energy

Understanding the specifics of the energy theory is the first and most important thing you should perform. Understanding the specifics of the energy theory is necessary if you want to manage your anger and bring it under control.

We'll provide you with some advice here that will undoubtedly be useful.

• Energy makes up every one of us.

• Energy particles simply keep changing from one segment to another because they are neither created nor destroyed.

- Maintaining a positive mental alignment is essential to reaching maximum achievement.

- Maintaining mental control is essential to aligning your ideas, and doing so requires a high degree of self-control.

- Certain energy particles move in a different direction when you are upset with someone. Additionally, it can start an energy collision that will cause chaos and bewilderment. Your inner serenity will be thwarted when your body's energy balance is out of control because this will only have bad effects. You'll probably encounter unpleasant circumstances since your body will be overflowing with bad energy, and you won't enjoy the response you receive.

Now that you are familiar with the basics of energy theory, we want you to consider how you might apply it to enhance your anger management techniques. We've broken down the tasks into easy steps that you should be able to follow without any difficulty.

1. Never start the day anything but happy. Try to greet it with a grin, no matter how difficult the day may be. Since it's said that the day begins in the morning, you should make sure that your energy particles are oriented optimally each morning.

2. It's important to take a step back and focus on the positive aspects of your life thus far whenever you see anything getting out of control. This is a crucial step because it helps to align the energy molecules in the correct direction when you surround your mind with positive ideas.

3. Deep breathing exercises should begin as soon as you sense the beginning of an angry outburst. Choosing to breathe deeply facilitates the articulate alignment of the energy particles. You can also take a seat and make an effort to clear your mind of any unfavorable ideas.

By doing these easy measures, you can align the positive energy and prevent rage.

Think things through.

Have you ever attempted to control your anger while being reasonable? You'll discover that most of the time, difficult-to-explain causes lead to rage. When circumstances don't turn out how we expected them to, viewing it as an irrational response is common. Therefore, talking things out is wiser than becoming upset and doing bad things for you or the other people involved.

The next time you feel irritated, sit and start looking around.

The things that infuriated you

b) Your part in the overall circumstance

d) Take responsibility for your actions.

d) Seek a cooperative resolution

e) Consider whether expressing anger would help you win your case; the answer is almost always no.

f) Construct a backup strategy.

With the help of this easy technique, you can manage your anger, and soon, you won't even experience rage.

Take part in productive activities.

Participating in various constructive exercises is another thing you may do to help deal with anger management.

Distracting yourself with a different subject is one of the finest strategies to deal with rage. Try to choose jobs requiring great concentration because you won't have time to get furious when working on them.

There are many activities available for you to select from. Simple activities like using a treadmill could occasionally be beneficial as well. Thus, you must comprehend what needs to be done. Selecting such productive activities will undoubtedly assist you in significantly reducing your levels of rage. You should attempt solving riddles if you have a flair for it. This will help you make better decisions by sharpening your intellect simultaneously.

Nothing good has ever come from being angry. Because of this, deciding to engage in constructive activities could prove to be a wise choice and a useful strategy for controlling anger.

You should employ some of the simplest yet highly powerful techniques listed here to help you control your anger. We want you to ensure you have implemented them before moving on with the book. If you've been successful, reaching your objective of effective anger management should be simpler.

One sign is an increase in blood flow to the brain and other parts of the body. Polyphenols, vitamin E, and omega-3 foods have been connected to blood flow. Among the foods that contain these ingredients are blueberries, red wine, and dark chocolate.

Recent research has also established a connection between the brain and a healthy digestive system. In particular, the gut microbiome can affect the brain and other body systems. Eating foods that promote a healthy microbiome include beans, veggies, yogurt, and cereals high in fiber.

#18 Reducing stress can also result from taking the time to "see the big picture". A person may experience periods when they are overburdened with several assignments and projects. While learning to say "no" to others can help reduce stress, other options exist when the tasks are all for one's benefit.

Some tension can be reduced when someone takes the time to stand back and consider everything that has to be done. To make the most of this trick, consider how crucial it is to complete the task at hand while focusing on the one that is now being worked on. Then, prioritize the remaining jobs by listing others that still need to be completed.

Once this is determined, it is time to prioritize the most critical project and put any tasks that do not require immediate attention on hold. For example, someone has a presentation to complete for a client. Making the presentation aesthetically beautiful would merely be a bonus; finishing the presentation is the main aim. Avoid giving undue attention to the non-essential component as this might cause unneeded stress and make it more difficult for the person to accomplish the actual activity or objective for which they started.

#19 One of the most crucial steps in managing stress levels is learning what makes one relax. Find what works best for you. It could be yoga, meditation, or gentle exercise. Speak to a family member or friend over the phone could also suffice.

When an individual determines the best approach, it's time to incorporate that approach into their daily routine. For instance, if someone thinks meditation is relaxing and enticing, they could dedicate fifteen minutes each night before bed to practicing meditation or listening to music before drifting off to sleep. Additionally, this may result in a better-controlled sleep schedule.

It's also crucial to remember not to take advice or suggestions from others for general solace at face value. It's important to remember what will help you relax the most—ask yourself. Everybody maintains their composure in different ways. As a result, what suits one individual may not suit another either.

#20 Discovering what makes you tranquil is similar to discovering what causes you to become more stressed. You should try to avoid these situations as much as possible. Take time to consider what stresses you out the most. Try choosing a different route with less traffic if, for instance, being caught in traffic on your way to work is one of your worst triggers.

Comprehending one's triggers might aid an individual in managing and overcoming stress. If someone can identify the situations that stress them out the most, they can list the triggers and eliminate them one at a time to reduce stress. For instance, someone can get anxious about not having enough time to get dressed before work in the morning rather than traffic. They could consider setting their alarm clock thirty minutes earlier to give themselves more time before work.

#21 Taking care of oneself comes first and is the unifying goal of all the stress-reduction techniques mentioned above. Diabetes is one of the health issues that can develop when someone allows stress to take control of their life.

The fundamental bodily processes that maintain health, including eating and sleeping, seem less significant in the face of extreme stress. Recent research, however, indicates that stress can be reduced by using basic human capabilities. For instance, a full night's sleep helps lower stress hormones and improve productivity.

As mentioned before, there are additional health advantages to eating a balanced diet. It extends beyond eating healthily, though. Because they believe they don't have enough time, some people decide not to eat at all. Additionally, be wary of foods with a high glycemic index as they may make someone feel much more hungry than they would have if they hadn't eaten. A person may get irritable and cause more stress to an already stressful day or scenario if they choose to eat items that make them feel hungry or if they are undereating.

An individual can become exhausted from the emotional and physical repercussions of stress, regardless of their level of preparation for it. Individuals who practice regular stress management techniques can prepare for known and unknown stressful circumstances.

How Does Anger Affect You?

Constant displays of anger might drive someone away from the workplace and their household. Nobody likes to be around someone who is constantly furious. People tend to avoid getting involved with this emotion, which can have long-lasting effects on the individual experiencing the anger and the one seeing it.

Try this if it's unclear enough: One letter separates anger from danger!

To be honest, most of us behave badly when we are furious, and we frequently say things that we later regret. Do you recall any incidents where somebody did or said something and then had to return and apologize? Thus, becoming angry is similar to being intoxicated in that the person experiencing the anger is the only one unaware that they are experiencing a problem.

What makes anger so harmful is its inherent nature. Is the fact that it can happen quickly and spiral out of control. The situation is out of your control before you even realize it, so the best way to reduce damage is to regain control—something many people frequently forget to do. To reduce it, we must comprehend what anger is and what triggers it.

What Leads to Anger Issues?

The only plausible explanation for our anger is when someone doesn't behave as we had anticipated. You say that's fascinating. Anger is an emotion rather than an action in and of itself, or more significantly, the outcome of an emotion. It is the response to the actions of another individual. Thus, becoming enraged is allowing someone else to dominate you. When did something positive come out of your anger last time?

The most typical expressions of anger are nonverbal and spoken.

It is evident that some people are offended by what others say, how they say it, or even the tone of their voice.

Additionally, non-verbal indicators such as tightening fists, glaring, frowning, and trying to appear physically larger and, therefore, scarier can be used to express anger. Some people are adept at internalizing their anger, so it could be challenging to recognize any physical symptoms. However, it is unusual for a genuine physical attack to occur without any initial "warning" signs.

Anger frequently arises from emotional situations that escalate and spiral out of control. Examine how children behave. They frequently lose their temper, have tantrums, and become hysterical. When a circumstance separates them, they typically experience this discomfort when they feel overlooked, unheard, or dismissed. They frequently lack the knowledge to communicate their emotions, which can lead to conflict as their frustration intensifies.

This situation can also be observed in adult behavior. An adult may well resort to rage to attract attention when they feel they have run out of options.

Potential Outward Symptoms of Anger:

There are frequently psychological and emotional signs of anger, and by identifying them, we increase our chances of managing them.

Possible Physical Indications of Anger:

- You regularly rub your face.

Tightly holding one hand over the other or clenching your fists.

• Teeth grinding or clenching of the jaw.

• Breathlessness or shallow breathing.

• An elevated heart rate.

• Sweaty, sweaty palms.

• Shaking hands or trembling lips.

• Rocking back and forth while seated.

• Pacing.

• Your sense of humor fades, and you start acting rudely.

• Your voice becomes louder; • You start to crave items that you believe could help you unwind, such as tobacco, cigarettes, alcohol, drugs, comfort food, etc.

Possible Anger Emotional Symptoms

• The desire to "run away" from the circumstances.

• Ritualization.

• Sensational or depressed.

• Feeling resentful or guilty.

• Feeling anxious can manifest itself in a variety of ways.

• A desire or mood to let go physically or sexually.

Let's Examine A Few of the Reasons Behind Anger Issues.

A youngster may exhibit learned furious behavior if they consistently use anger as a coping mechanism for frustration or dissatisfaction, typically at home. When an individual exhibits dissatisfaction and disagreement more frequently than is typical, particularly in their formative years, overcoming this reaction and discovering more effective and positive methods of handling issues may be challenging. Some individuals acquire the ability to accept becoming angry as the typical response; others may create a tense environment and become afraid of opposing viewpoints or disagreements, becoming quiet and reserved to avoid any argument.

One characteristic of an angry scenario is frequent disregard. When someone else makes them feel foolish, unappreciated, or undermined, they frequently don't know what to do. Sometimes, even if it means shoving and creating a hostile environment, that individual may feel that any attention is preferable to none and will try to be noticed.

• Fruit. A person may develop the belief that, no matter what they do or how hard they try, they will always be perceived negatively. Continuously striving to better oneself and being driven enough to want to improve and inspire others might be discouraging if the results are always the same. They can think that their efforts aren't being sufficiently appreciated, that they don't receive the same recognition as others, or that they don't seem to be getting good prospects.

• Inadequate communication skills, particularly when exhibited by someone perceived as highly educated and artistic, might cause a person to become reticent and uncertain about what to say. This person may gradually lose confidence, their sense of self-worth may be diminished, and they may come to believe that they are incapable of speaking enough to be understood. Even worse, they could think what they say will be interpreted as foolish, unclear, or poorly phrased.

- Bullying situations occasionally provoke angry reactions. A victim of long-term bullying frequently loses the ability to express their circumstances. They could feel weak, afraid, like it's their fault, or like they're somehow flawed. Individual bullying experiences might often seem insignificant, or the victims believe they should be able to handle the situation on their own effectively. Anger may eventually explode when the strain mounts, and they are determined to resolve the situation.

- Losing can make you angry. Some people lack the necessary tools to deal with failure or rejection. They might have always been successful; they might have been a golden child who excelled in everything. Losing out can be an unfamiliar scenario in which they lack the necessary skills to cope. A tantrum and displaying anger could be a reaction to the situation's unfamiliarity and a sign that they don't have the resources to deal with it.

Anger frequently stems from feeling helpless or powerless over what is happening. It is critical to understand how to remain composed, to identify what's happening, and to understand why it affects us. After that, we can decide what has to be done to improve the situation and identify appropriate channels for communicating our feelings. While it may take some time, this is a crucial step in developing into a responsible adult.

Restructuring cognition

To put it simply, this is changing your way of thinking. Angry people tend to use profanity, swear, or speak in highly colorful words that convey their inner feelings. Your thoughts may become overly dramatic and overblown when you're angry. Try swapping these out for more logical concepts.

Avoid "never" or "always" while discussing yourself or others. Not only are statements like "this machine never works" or "you're constantly forgetting things" incorrect, but they also contribute to the idea that you have good reason to be angry and that there is nothing you can do about it. They also degrade and alienate people who otherwise want to work with you to find a solution.

Remember that being upset won't improve everything and can make you feel worse. If anything, it will only make you feel worse.

Reason prevails over wrath because, even in justified cases, rage can quickly become irrational. Therefore, use rational thinking on oneself. Remind yourself that you are going through difficult times and that the world is "not out to get you." Try doing this whenever you feel your wrath is getting the best of you; it will give you a more impartial perspective.

Angry people often want fairness, respect, cooperation, and the willingness to fulfill their wishes. Everyone wants these things, and we're all hurt and disappointed when we don't get them. However, furious people demand these things, and their disappointment turns into rage when their expectations aren't met.

Anger-prone people must learn to recognize their demanding behavior and transform their expectations into wishes as part of their cognitive restructuring. Stated differently, it is preferable to say

"I would like" something as opposed to "I demand" or "I must have" something. You won't become furious when you don't get what you want; instead, you will experience the normal emotions of hurt, disappointment, and frustration. Some angry people use their anger as a coping mechanism for hurt feelings, but this doesn't mean suffering disappears.

Solving issues

Sometimes, our natural and unavoidable difficulties set off our rage and frustration. Anger is not always misplaced; it's a legitimate response to these situations in many cases. Additionally, there is a social belief that there is always a solution to a problem, which makes us even more unhappy when we learn this isn't always the case. Therefore, the best mindset in such a situation is to focus on how you approach and address the problem rather than trying to figure out the solution.

Create a plan and evaluate your progress as you go. Decide to give it your all, but don't hold yourself responsible if you don't hear back immediately.

Improved dialogue

Furious people sometimes jump to conclusions and act upon them, even though some of those conclusions may be gravely incorrect. When engaged in a heated argument, the first thing to do is to gather yourself and consider your remarks. Instead of speaking at the first thing that comes to mind, take a moment to gather your thoughts and carefully consider what you want to say. Simultaneously, pay great attention to what the other person is saying and wait to respond.

Pay attention to the source of the anger as well. For example, while your "significant other" wants closer proximity and more connection, you want independence and privacy. Don't respond to a spouse complaining about your actions by painting them as a warden, a jailer, or an albatross around your neck.

It's common to feel defensive in the face of criticism but refrain from retaliating. Rather, pay attention to the message underlying the words: this person may feel undesired and abandoned. You may need to ask many pointed questions and give yourself some space, but don't let your or your partner's rage cause a disagreement to get out of hand. Remaining composed could prevent the situation from getting worse.

erratic fury

This is the specific type of rage that seems to come out of nowhere.

Generally speaking, people get angry over everything, no matter how tiny. This kind of rage nearly always subsides quickly when it is voiced impulsively.

Regretfully, rage of this nature has a very negative tendency. This is because those in your immediate vicinity will feel compelled to avoid you out of concern that you might incite wrath. Negative reactions could arise from this condition if it is not treated.

To deal with this rage, you must carefully identify the symptoms and indicators accompanying these outbursts to deal with how you can utilize relaxation techniques to properly manage your anger so it doesn't escalate, build up to a boiling point, and finally blow up.

ANGER AS A REPLACEMENT FOR EMOTION

Did you know that rage can serve as a stand-in emotion on occasion? "But what do you mean by a substitute emotion?" one may wonder. Indeed, there are instances when people push themselves into a rage to avoid facing their suffering. This implies that since it feels better to be furious than to be in pain, you choose to replace your suffering with anger rather than letting yourself grieve it away. This could occur inadvertently or on purpose.

There are many benefits to feeling fury rather than pain, but the primary one is diversion. When you're hurting, your pain consumes all of your thoughts. But when you're upset, it's simple to consider hurting the people who have hurt you. Stated differently, there is a change in attention from self-centeredness to social awareness.

It is crucial to understand that rage only serves as a temporary shield to prevent people from realizing, addressing, and overcoming their intense emotions. All of a sudden, you have to think about getting even. One thing to remember, though, is that allowing yourself to become furious is essential to helping you conceal the fact that the scenario you are facing is terrifying and makes you feel exposed.

Not only can anger serve as a sufficient smoke screen for vulnerability, but it also engenders sentiments of power, righteousness, and moral superiority—elements lacking in pain. To put it briefly, you have a reason to be furious when you are angry. Put another way, when you're upset, your thoughts are filled with the idea that the people who have hurt you should be held accountable. Stated differently, it is rare to encounter someone who is not enraged with someone who has not harmed them somehow.

So, what are the advantages and disadvantages of anger?

Even though rage is a bad emotion, it has several positive social, health, and emotional aspects. Whether or not your wrath is warranted, that alluring sense of righteousness gives our egos a stronger boost and calms us down.

Acknowledging the uncomfortable sensation of vulnerability is frequently more satisfying than being outraged. Put differently, you can leverage your anger to transform helplessness and vulnerability into control and power. Some people find it helpful to establish an unconscious habit of turning their vulnerable emotions into rage to avoid confronting the true problems.

The issue with this behavior pattern is that even though anger makes you more resistant to vulnerability—the truth—you are still somewhat exposed. Put another way, just because you become angry doesn't guarantee your suffering will disappear overnight. You are only momentarily distracted from it by it.

13. Anger that Abuses Oneself:

Anger that is self-abusive is generally connected to shame or humiliation. People with low self-esteem or feelings of helplessness and hopelessness tend to become angry in this way. Self-abusive rage is typically adopted as a coping mechanism for these emotions, even if it just serves to push people away.

Anger that is self-abusive can affect you both within and outside. It might manifest as internalizing bad emotions and taking them out on oneself, such as by self-harming actions, abusing alcohol or drugs, eating unhealthily or undesired foods, or engaging in negative self-talk (such as "You are a failure."). From the outside, this can appear to be striking out, pursuing, or verbally assaulting others.

14. Manipulative Fury:

Rage manipulation can resemble chronic rage in many ways. It is employed as an aware or unaware control method over other people.

Manipulative rage is frequently loud and erratic, just like explosive rage. The idea is to startle everyone in your vicinity into obeying.

Eventually, of course, these attempts at control will fail because your targets will just put up with a great deal of chaos before departing.

15. Quiet Fury:

Another term for silent rage is non-verbal anger or an inward expression of wrath. While you might not say it out loud, others can infer you are upset. Silent anger sufferers frequently suppress their emotions and let them grow, which can lead to increased strain, tension, and overwhelmed anger-related behavior.

Anger that remains silent can come from the within or the outside. This kind of rage within can build into unspoken dissatisfaction, rage, and contempt, leading to high pressure and low levels of increasing tension. On the outside, it may appear as restricted or inconsequential speech and tone, as well as inhibited nonverbal cues and facial expressions.

16. Verbal Fury:

Anger that is expressed verbally can be strong and overwhelming. After striking out at their target, those who experience this kind of fury are known to feel regret and may even attempt an apology.

Anger that is expressed verbally can have the appearance of "going off" or erupting on someone. Examples of explicit behaviors include yelling, undermining behaviors, sardonic remarks, continuous and severe criticism, and scorning. Keep in mind that verbal abuse can develop from verbal rage. It may also prevent maintaining consistent, stable, or healthy relationships.

17. Anger in Retaliation:

An automatic and common response to being attacked is retaliatory rage. It could easily be influenced by a desire for vengeance following a perceived wrong.

Usually, the target of this kind of rage is someone who has intentionally wounded you. It usually gets affected by having to deal with an event. It's possible that you will eventually become enraged with someone after experiencing verbal or physical abuse. Relationship tension and fury may increase when there is retaliatory wrath.

Does Getting Furious Affect the Circumstance?

Indeed, experiencing anger can positively and negatively affect our lives. We have two types of rage: "constructive anger" and "destructive anger." Our acts during an angry outburst can either cause constructive or destructive fury. The following are a few ways that rage can alter our lives:

1. Anger might force you to give up bad habits.

Bad behaviors have the power to make you feel self-conscious. You might become enraged over this and decide to break these bad habits. Your motivation to kick unhealthy habits and adopt healthy ones will come from your anger, and as a result, your life will improve.

2. Anger can strengthen bonds in interpersonal relationships.

When one partner constructively expresses anger towards another on certain issues in a relationship, the two can get down and work out a solution. However, peaceful, polite resolution of these conflicts is the only option available; combative approaches, such as yelling and assigning blame, are never appropriate.

3. Anger has the power to advance your career.

Anger might be brought on by unfair treatment or feeling undervalued at work. Perhaps due to your different academic standing, you may feel your peers are demeaning you. If someone uses their anger constructively, it might inspire them to put in more effort and pursue their education. This will help him or her land a better position.

Does the Way Men and Women Handle Anger Differ? If so, why?

All people experience anger, but because of gender socialization, the way we show that anger can vary depending on our gender. Males are known for using violent methods to release their frustration, which might include yelling at their spouses, girlfriends, or even coworkers. However, if a man consumes alcohol, he can go out with buddies and vent his feelings.

Conversely, women will just practice breathing in and out or spend a moment alone to calm down when irritated. Since society views women as peacemakers, many of them are raised to learn how to control their anger and behave peacefully; as a result, openly displaying rage is seen as a sign that a woman is not sufficiently feminine or well-mannered.

Ladies can mask their suffering with a false grin. Although they may appear calm and cozy, they could be roasting on the inside. They typically hold their anger longer than males because societal shame prevents them from expressing it aggressively.

Gender roles are imposed by culture on how we express our emotions in our society. However, regardless of gender, expressing anger is crucial since it promotes healing more quickly and is generally healthy. Anger management issues include tension, ulcerative stomach, elevated blood pressure, and even stroke, which can result from holding onto anger. Conflict is inevitable in daily life, whether at work or at home. Women should be taught that it's acceptable to express their anger rather than holding it inside.

The anatomical characteristics of men's and women's brains provide a different explanation for how differently men and women regulate their anger, according to science. According to research, men's brains develop and mature more slowly than women's. They contend that men's brains have smaller portions than women's that control aggression, which explains why men are more likely than women to express their emotions in violent ways. Additionally, a woman's brain processes information faster than a man's.

Men tend to act without thinking, which explains why they are more prone to get into conflicts and participate in risky behavior. Women are controlled by estrogen, which makes it easier for their minds to resolve problems, even if it means sacrificing their positions. For this reason, women always put others before themselves.

Contrarily, testosterone hormones govern men and cause them to be aggressive to compete, assert their dominance, and assert their authority. This explains why they become enraged easily in any kind of disagreement. Men and women differ physiologically, and these distinctions have benefits and drawbacks.

In an attempt to motivate their employees to perform better, many managers tend to use furious outbursts. While rage can serve as a motivator in the workplace, an individual's productivity may suffer if they experience fits of rage frequently.

If you frequently lose your temper at work, this can be detrimental to your career in several ways:

• You can start to feel anger towards your supervisor or coworkers.

• If you cannot be disabled, anger may harm your reputation.

• Your coworkers might think you're an abusive person.

- If you inappropriately display your anger in the workplace, you might be the target of a lawsuit.

- It's possible that your coworkers won't cooperate with you.

- Your managers might not include you in important projects because they don't think you can complete them well enough.

- You might lose business or consumers.

- Your employment could be terminated.

You can learn more healthy coping mechanisms for handling anger when it arises with the correct skill set and counseling.

Take Responsibility for Your Anger

Taking ownership of our emotions is one of the most prevalent issues that affect everyone on some level. When we feel bad, we usually try to take it out on other people and find someone to blame. Upon experiencing hurt, we blame the other person and immediately start planning to get revenge on them.

How often have you heard guys attack their partners during tense arguments by saying things like, "I wouldn't have hit her if she hadn't talked back at me like that"? Or when someone becomes angry on the road because they think another driver has offended them, does that mean "he deserves to be beaten because he cut me off"?

In actuality, humans tend to have a warped view of who we are—that is, to see ourselves as victims and others as evil entities out to get us. But in the long term, this incorrect perception simply causes trouble since it keeps us from accepting accountability for our feelings.

Our upbringing is the source of our inclination to hold others responsible for our feelings. The majority of persons who place the blame for misfortune on others may have picked up this habit by watching the reactions of their caregivers. When something goes wrong, and a kid's parents or other caregivers tend to avoid taking responsibility, the youngster will likely pick up these behaviors and carry them into adulthood. In other cases, trauma is typically the cause. If someone has received constant criticism or mockery for accepting accountability, they could be more likely to assign blame to avoid dealing with their unpleasant feelings.

Whatever the situation, assigning blame to others for our feelings, including anger, is a defensive mechanism that needs to be conquered to develop a constructive anger management plan.

Refusing to take accountability can help you save face in the near term, but it also has bad effects that can seriously harm your relationships and health.

Blaming other people for your anger can prevent you from controlling it in the following ways:

● It Could Keep Someone From Realizing Their Own Worth

Blaming other people all the time for how you control your anger can seriously undermine one's self-esteem. This is because assigning blame leads to the impression that an individual is a victim dependent on others. One's power is diminished by this skewed perception, which can cause emotions of helplessness and exacerbate rage and aggression. Because they believe other people are accountable for their decisions, people who adopt this victimhood image also forfeit their independence, making them more likely to become angry.

● Relationship Dependency May Result from It

Anger-mongers cannot accept accountability for their behaviors, feelings, and lives. They constantly depend on others to make choices for them and boost their self-esteem. Because an irresponsible person needs someone to blame when angry, this unwillingness to accept responsibility for rage frequently results in dependent relationships.

● It Prevents Introspection

Self-awareness is a crucial quality for controlling one's anger. It enables one to objectively evaluate circumstances and draw appropriate conclusions free from the influence of one's prejudices and emotions. But when someone is always blaming others for their anger, they stop seeing their reflections and critique of themselves. Consequently, they develop fictitious narratives and perceptions of other individuals in their minds. This exacerbates their anger management issues because they start to harshly criticize other people and believe that they are the source of their rage.

While shifting blame can help someone avoid accepting responsibility for their anger, doing so simply worsens their problems because it becomes a habit and makes them always angry.

● It Causes Helplessness Feelings

Since it makes you feel like a victim all the time, blaming other people for your anger might make you feel uncomfortable and helpless. If not dealt with immediately, this could result in despair and a never-ending cycle of rage.

● It Hinders Personal Growth and Advancement

Blaming others for one's anger can lead to a victimhood mindset, which can be extremely harmful to one's personal development. This is because it impedes the growth of traits like resilience, tolerance, and patience. Therefore, someone who continually places the blame for their rage elsewhere is not likely to handle life's little setbacks very well.

While it would seem simple to continually place the responsibility for our anger on others, adopting a victim mindset does not offer sustainable strategies for controlling our fury. It robs us of our independence and the joy and liberty of taking responsibility for our actions. Therefore, we must stop this tendency and start realizing the part our emotions play in our lives.

Of course, starting ownership of our rage might not be simple. If we unintentionally picked up this habit as kids, it could be quite challenging to recognize it for what it is and take the appropriate action to break it. However, if we want to better our lives and our relationships, we all need to work toward accepting responsibility for our anger.

Manage Your Anger Before It Takes Over You

Anger might make you feel powerless in the face of a strong, flighty impulse. Determine a way to manage it.

How to Manage Your Anger

We all know what anger is, and we've all experienced it, whether it takes the form of a fleeting annoyance or an uncontrollable rage. Anger is a perfectly normal, healthy human tendency. However, if it becomes uncontrollable and out of control, it can lead to problems in your relationships, career, and overall quality of life.

Anger might make you feel powerless in the face of a strong, unusual inclination.

Communicating Anger

Answering angrily is the automatic, habitual way to express anger. Anger is a normal, adaptable response to threats; it elicits powerful, often violent feelings and behaviors that enable us to defend and fight back when pursued. Thus, a certain level of anger is necessary for our perseverance.

Nevertheless, there are limits to how far our rage may drive us due to laws, social norms, and the presence of the mind; we cannot truly assault every person or thing that annoys or upsets us.

People use several cycles—both conscious and unconscious—to control their angry feelings. Suppressing, Calming, and Expressing are the three main approaches. The greatest approach to showing anger is to do so in a decisive manner that avoids using force. You must determine your needs and how to satisfy them without endangering other people to do this. Being self-assured means understanding yourself and others; it does not imply being demanding or aggressive.

One can control one's anger and then redirect or change it later. This is the result of suppressing your rage, giving up worrying about anything, and focusing on the good. The goal is to smother or suppress your hate and turn it into a more constructive behavior. This type of response carries the risk that, in the unlikely event that overt displays of disapproval are prohibited, your anger may become internalized against you. Internalized anger can result in depression, high blood pressure, or hypertension.

Unspoken anger might lead to several problems. It can cause neurotic expressions of rage, such as a character who appears perpetually gloomy and menacing or an uninvolved, strong manner of behaving (retaliating against people deviously without giving them a reason). People who constantly criticize everything put down other people, and make negative comments haven't learned constructive ways to express their displeasure. They most likely won't have as many strong ties as one might anticipate.

You may finally relax on the inside. This means managing your behavior on the outside and your internal responses. You must take all necessary steps to lower your heart rate, regain your composure, and allow your emotions to pass.

Dr.Spielberger states, "When none of these three methods work, that is the point at which somebody or something will get injured."

Controlling Your Anger

Reducing your emotional reactions and the physical agitation that comes with rage is the aim of anger management. You can't get rid of or avoid the things or people who irritate you, nor can you ever change them, but you can learn how to manage your reactions.

Do you feel that you are too angry?

The tests of the mind gauge the intensity of your anger, your propensity for resentment, and your ability to control it. Regardless, chances are high that you are aware of it, presuming you detest fury. If you find yourself behaving in ways that seem insane and frightening, you may need help finding more effective ways to deal with this tendency.

For what reason do some people have more rage than others?

According to Jerry Deffenbacher, Ph. D., a clinician with practical experience in Anger Management, some people are just plain "rash"; they get angry faster and more intensely than the average person. Others are often irritable and short-tempered but don't express their displeasure in overtly dramatic ways. Those who are easily enraged don't always detest and discard things; occasionally, they withdraw socially, pout, or become ill.

Effectively enraged people, for the most part, have what some doctors call a low capacity to take disappointment, which means they believe they shouldn't have to deal with anger, worry, or aggravation. They cannot accept things and get quite irrational when the situation seems out of character—for example, when they are made whole for a small mistake.

WHAT CONVICES THESE PEOPLE TO FALL IN LINE? Different stuff. One explanation could be physiological or genetic: There is evidence that certain children are born with a short fuse, are cunning, and are easily enraged, and these traits are present from a young age. Sociocultural factors could be another. Fury is frequently associated with pessimism; we've been taught that showing tension, discouragement, or other emotions is acceptable, but not fury. As a result, we are unable to handle or direct it effectively.

Studies have also revealed that familial foundation plays a role. Those who are easily irritated typically originate from unruly, unstable households and lack in-depth communication skills.

Is "letting everything hang out" a great idea?

These days, therapists describe this as a dangerous delusion. Some people use this theory as an excuse to harm other people. According to research, "allowing it to tear" with rage only serves to intensify the anger and hostility between you and the person you're angry with, and it never truly helps to find a solution.

It's best to identify what exactly triggers your annoyance and then create mechanisms to prevent those triggers from pushing you over the brink.

Strategies For Controlling Outrage

Relaxing

It can be a good idea for both of you to become familiar with these techniques if you are in a relationship with a lot of resentment between the partners.

Here are a few simple moves you can try:

PROFOUNDLY BLOW FROM YOUR STOMACH: Breathing from your chest won't make you more relaxed. Visualize the breath rising from your "gut."Repeat a calm word or phrase slowly, like "unwind" or "relax." Breathe deeply and repeat it to yourself. Use symbols; picture a relaxing meeting in your mind or your recollections. Slow, gentle yoga-style exercises will help you feel much more at ease and loosen up your muscles.

Use these techniques daily. Learn how to use them appropriately when faced with a difficult situation.

Restructuring Cognitively

This means changing the way you think all the way around. People who are angry frequently despise, curse, or use extremely vivid language that reflects their inner thoughts. When angry, you may think in a very dynamic and misleading way. Try substituting some extra objective factors for these. For example, remind yourself, "It's baffling, and it's justifiable that I'm unglued about it. However, it's not the apocalypse, and blowing up won't fix it in any case," instead of, "Gracious, it's horrendous, it's awful, everything's destroyed."

When talking about yourself or someone else, words like "never" or "consistently" should be avoided. Not only are statements like "this machine never works" or "you're constantly forgetting things" false, but they also give you the impression that your anger is justified and that solving the problem is virtually unachievable. They also alienate and humiliate those who might be able to collaborate with you on a solution.

Remind yourself that losing your cool won't make things better or inspire you; it can make things worse.

Justification calms anger because, even when it is justified, fury can quickly turn into a ridiculous situation. So, apply the hard logic to yourself. Tell yourself that the world is "not on a mission to get you" and that you are just experiencing some of the difficult moments that come with living your daily life. Do this every time you feel your wrath getting the better of you. It will help you gain a more perspective. Usually, angry people would ask for kindness, gratitude, comprehension, and the willingness to carry out their wishes. These are necessities for everyone, and we are hurt and annoyed when we don't receive them. Nevertheless, enraged people ask for these things, and when their demands are denied, their inadequacy is viewed as outrageous.

Anger management requires that angry people learn to recognize when making demands and translate their assumptions into wants as part of their mental reconstruction. Overall, expressing "I would like" as opposed to "I am interested" or "I should have" is more realistic. When you cannot obtain what you require, you will experience the usual reactions, which include hurt, anger, and discontent but not outrage. Some enraged people use this irritation to avoid feeling wounded, but it doesn't imply the hurt disappears.

Recognizing the Different Types of Anger

Anger is a relatively common human emotion. It might be advantageous since it can help us identify problems in our personal and relationship lives and motivate us to take action to better our lives, those we love, and the lives of others. According to the study, there are 12 distinct forms of rage, which can be categorized into different spectrums and levels. Understanding the origin and nature of your anger is an essential first step toward controlling and managing it.

Inert Anger

People tend to avoid this type of rage the most, yet it can also irritate those around them. It demonstrates their dysfunctional relationship to this emotion and their belief that it is wrong, immoral, or improper in some other way for a person to feel. Some childhood experiences, such as being forced to repress all negative emotions, maybe the cause of it. This type of rage maybe even more emotionally and physically draining for the individual expressing it than more obvious ones. It can be expressed by sarcasm, delaying, mockery, or quiet treatment.

Instead of expressing their anger directly, some people use passive-aggressive techniques to hurt and confuse their victims. Most people will, at some point, deal with passive hostility from others in their personal and professional lives. Two examples are the endearing yet stern note from a roommate about the one cup that wasn't cleaned or the report that a colleague keeps "forgetting" to finish. Persistent or angry behavior only puts the passive-aggressive person on the defensive, frequently resulting in them apologizing or downplaying their guilt.

Aggressive anger

When someone is trying to dominate, intimidate, manipulate, or control another, they frequently use aggressive fury. When aggressive anger is consistently shown in relationships, it can develop into oppression, bullying, psychological violence, and emotional abuse. While this type of fury seems intense initially, it frequently hides a person's inner fears. Someone who exhibits violent outbursts of rage regularly could be trying to conceal from us a deep sense of fear and inadequacy. They can also try to control others to cover up their flaws and shortcomings.

Confident Fury

Aggressive anger is defined as anger that is expressed assertively. Instead of dodging confrontations or frequently yelling or screaming, assertive anger is used as a healthy and productive manner to express annoyance and effect positive change. The appearance of forceful fury could be an excellent, safe way to communicate your feelings. For example, you could start a sentence with "I think..." or "I feel furious when..."

In addition to appropriate body language, assertive rage is frequently accompanied by expectations about how to respond to or process the situation. You can now release your resentment in a way that promotes positive transformation.

Assertive rage provides the capacity to take control of one's situation and deal with the issue causing the anger. Because it's a more civil and mature way to express rage, it turns an unpleasant and challenging conflict situation into one that can be resolved. Where everyone actively looks for a solution and knows what the basis of the problem is. Assertive fury is preferable to aggressive or passive anger when outcomes and solutions come about by luck rather than from a position of control.

Furious people who employ aggressive anger management techniques respect both themselves and those around them rather than simply snapping or repressing their feelings, which could result in unresolved issues down the road that could have a long-term impact or conflict.

ImpactOf Anger

Is it ever going to be good?

You frequently come across passages that seem to suggest that there are situations in which rage is appropriate. that it could be used ingeniously to accomplish certain beneficial objectives. How did they acquire this odd belief?

Leading Greek scholar Aristotle proposed two millennia ago that individuals could reduce stress by acting in ways that could come out as negative. He defined "catharsis" as the process by which an individual can reestablishemotional equilibrium after viewing a tragic drama.

According to Aristotle, acting out anger instead of holding it inside would allow people to release emotional tension and experience psychological tranquility.

As time went on, Austrian neurologist Sigmund Freud expanded on the catharsis theory of rage, arguing that suppressed anger would eventually lead to psychiatric disorders. People were encouraged to express their rage.

Recent research has demonstrated that Freud and Aristotle were both incorrect. To paraphrase Carol Tavris, we need to "shoot a hole straight through the heart of the belief that venting violence will eliminate hostilities in people's minds."

The truth is that people who behave out of anger in an attempt to feel better about themselves ultimately wind up feeling much more resentment. They continue digging further into the anger's quicksand and suffer the consequences. Poisoned words or deeds can never bring good.

It's inappropriate to take a strong stance against people who cross your boundaries in the hopes of achieving mental tranquility. You'd want to cool off. To settle disputes, control your emotions, and have meaningful conversations with others. A peaceful resolution will ensure that all parties are satisfied and can return home less stressed.

Negative consequences of fury

Rage, indeed, has no positive aspects. Instead, a higher risk of heart disease, depression, gastrointestinal issues, and high blood pressure has been associated with rage, according to studies and clinical observation.

Anger has also been connected to stroke, chronic anxiety, insomnia, and skin conditions. You conclude that rage is one fatal vector that must be avoided at all costs.

In this section of the manual, we'll look at just five of the numerous ways that anger can negatively impact the health of those prone to it.

It endangers your heart.

No question that being angry can be harmful to your heart. After adjusting for all other variables, a study by North Carolina physician and clinical psychiatry instructor Chris Aiken revealed that those with higher impulsivity were twice as likely to develop a cardiac condition as their less irascible counterparts.

Additionally, it was stated that in at-risk individuals, the likelihood of experiencing a heart attack doubles in the two hours following a furious outburst. Thus, consider the dangers to your heart health before you blow hot.

Anger Guards Our Principles And Ideas

Anger serves as a vehicle for expressing and controlling one's social and private interests. It is set off when our beliefs don't match our circumstances. As a result, it helps us remember our core beliefs and principles. It also spurs us to make amends, act to alter the circumstances (or our beliefs), and bring the reality we encounter into compliance with our values.

Anger Is A Tool For Bargaining

Anger will unavoidably surface when someone places less importance or value on your health. Anger is meant to raise our curiosity by recalibrating the situation. Wrath can encourage others to comply with our position and amply support it. Anger forces us to react to conflict in a way that advances our interests through compromise. This causes other people to second-guess their choices. On the other hand, this indicates that you should be able to modify the amount you distribute to me to lower my expenses or provide value because what you are proposing is too hazardous for me.

Anger Promotes Collaboration

Anger says, "I don't like the situation, and we must work together to find a better way out." Anger makes you stand up and challenge the other side constructively, which is how anger fosters teamwork. If anger is justified and the response is appropriate, the mistake is usually resolved, and the support is improved.

Anger Strengthens Positions in Negotiation

Anger is a negotiating tool used to persuade, reach an agreement, or strengthen the agreed position. It has been observed that business negotiations yield better results when the parties are angry. The angrier the negotiator appears, the more likely they may be to reject the deal in their favor, as two parties compromise.

Anger Is a Mask for Painful Emotions

Anger serves this essential psychological function, much as Sigmund Freud's defense mechanisms protect the individual against an overwhelming fear when the ego is threatened. Anger is a primal, "superficial" emotion that prevents you from feeling more painful feelings (defends / blocks). For instance, a person their partner has deceived may use rage to manipulate them rather than share their difficult-to-bear suffering.

Anger Forces Us to Explore Our Deeper Selves

A volcano is formed when magma pushes down the earth's crust from below and spews lava on top. Similarly, other powers, like terror and resistance, bring wrath to the surface. It could be fear of losing control or being alone, rejected, lost, unloved, etc. Fear offers insight into ourselves because it is the most hidden component of deeper issues. For this reason, it is important to map the path of wrath and work through the blockage that leads to rage. Only then can we get rid of the pain that anger occasionally causes?

Anger Can Help You Become a Better Person

Using anger constructively can have positive effects, and unlike inspiration, it can change itself. For example, once you know these things, you should rely on certain factors to enhance your reaction and strengthen your response, improving your quality of life and relationships. Anger will make you a stronger person and a catalyst for social change. It gives us insight into our flaws and shortcomings.

Experiencing Fury Boosts Emotional Intelligence

Those who are willing to accept and even welcome negative emotions like anger are more emotionally intelligent than those who resist or control them. Rather than fighting frustration, emotionally intelligent people use their "wisdom" to achieve their desired outcomes, which makes their emotional response systems remarkably resilient and effective.

Despite a negative history, researchers have provided more empirical evidence in favor of the idea that positive frustration can be constructive. Anger inspires us to act in ways that will help us accomplish our goals and correct the mistakes we observe in the universe.

Extreme anger works well in life-threatening situations but is never useful in everyday situations. The key to its effectiveness is that frustration is communicated with the necessary force, which allows us to sense it (rather than repress it) and use it sensibly. As Aristotle once said, "with the right person and at the right level."

Emotion can be likened to a spark or the primary force. It can cause havoc if rampant, but if controlled and employed wisely, it can be an invaluable and potent instrument that aids enlightenment.

Getting Medical Assistance

While some people might find it easy to learn to manage and control their anger on their own, it is quite complicated for others, and all they need to do is seek professional help for their issues. There are different anger management classes that a person who has anger issues could attend, and some might choose to go for private counseling sessions. If you have tried to learn to manage anger on your own, but you still have anger issues, it is a sign that your anger issue is profound and needs more than just trying to learn on your own. People with a chronic type of anger must especially go for medical help because chronic anger is not something you can learn to manage on your own. Also, as a person with Intermittent Explosive Disorder (IED), you should seek medical help instead of trying to manage your anger by yourself. Once you recognize that anger negatively affects your life, the best thing to do is seek medical help. Here are three of the methods by which you can seek medical help;

Personal Counseling

One way to get help for anger is to attend an individual counseling session. You will learn strategies and tactics to help you control your anger, and you will be able to practice in your therapist's company. Depending on your consistency, a high-level angry person can reduce their anger to a mid-range level in 8 to 10 weeks of therapy. For your counseling sessions to be truly effective, you must attend every appointment; you cannot schedule an appointment online or through your local hospital.

Group Counseling

People who suffer from similar anger disorders come together in groups and are allowed to express their feelings and listen to one another. There are many advantages to group therapy, some of which include the following: the chance to grow personally, the realization that you are not alone in the struggle to learn anger control, and knowing this will keep you motivated; group therapists are typically led by one or two therapists who guide the patients through each session; collectively, everyone in the group can learn techniques by which they can know how to manage and control their anger more effectively.

Going to a Support Group

Support groups are typically associations of people with a common goal, such as anger management, and are organized by the community. A support group can benefit you because it allows you to meet people who have been through a similar phase in life. It can also connect you with people who can offer support or struggle with similar anger management. In a support group, you can share your successes and struggles with others and receive and give excellent advice.

Enroll in a Course on Anger Management

People with anger disorders can find many community service organizations and mental health clinics that offer anger management classes. These classes can run for one night, a weekend, or weeks. You can register for these classes at a low cost or even for free. The theory and information covered in these classes is more than what they teach. You can learn about anger management classes in your area or sign up online.

Step 3: Channel Your Feelings of Anger and Dissatisfaction

It's time to tap into your experience of irritation and rage and use mindfulness to bring compassion and calmness to it now that you have a better awareness of the triggers and negative thought patterns that make you angry.

This provides you the courage to face your anger triggers and remain composed in their presence, as well as assist you in gradually calming down and releasing the anger that has accumulated inside you over the years.

Here's how to go about doing that.

1. Make yourself comfortable

Remove all sources of distraction, such as the television, laptop, and other devices that could divert you from this exercise, and find a quiet, peaceful place to sit.

Place your hands comfortably on your lap or by your sides, close your eyes, and sit comfortably in a chair or anyplace else you choose. The important thing to remember is that you should be aware of yourself and the current moment, even though you are sitting comfortably.

Take note of how your body feels and the various points on your body that are in contact with the cushion or chair you have been sitting on. This step and those that follow should take three to five minutes, but you are free to extend the time if you like.

2. Breathe deeply

Take deep breaths for around three minutes. To do this, fill your torso to the fullest for five counts, hold your breath for five counts, and then release it gradually for another five counts.

3. Recall a Time in the Past When You Were Angry.

Choose a recent memory in which you were very angry. You don't have to choose the worst instance; just go with whatever comes to mind. Start with a smaller, less volatile memory to help you stay calm in the moment. Recalling negative experiences can also make you angry, so starting with something less volatile is a good idea.

Imagine what was happening then and feel the situation again. Give yourself permission to feel the anger, hurt, and pain you felt then, and let that sensation intensify as far as it can without going to the point where you feel things are getting out of control.

Remember that an unpleasant experience is likely to bring up additional feelings like fear or grief, but for the time being, focus exclusively on the anger itself because that's what you're trying to calm.

4: Examine Your Body

Examine your body as you recall that unpleasant experience. Is there a particularly tense area? If so, explore and learn more about that area to understand what happens to your body when you get angry. For example, you may notice a rising temperature in your head or a burning sensation in your abdomen.

5: Empathize with Your Fury

Next, apply empathy and compassion to your angry and frustrated sentiments. Rather than criticizing yourself for being upset, realize that anger is a natural emotion everyone shares.

Since emotion helps you deal with difficult situations and grow from them, it is not inherently bad. But you should acknowledge that you have allowed this intense emotion to become harmful and persistent.

Give your anger a color, and then visualize a large ball of that color standing before you. That ball is your anger. For example, I visualize an orange ball of fury when I do this technique. This will help you bring compassion to your rage.

This ball should be wrapped in a blanket and held like a baby. It should be lovingly caressed like a mother would a newborn. You will eventually feel empathy for your anger if you keep seeing this.

6: Say Goodbye to This Emotion

Imagine opening your arms and releasing that ball of rage as soon as you feel your anger starting to subside. Then, very slowly, return your attention to your breathing.

Pay attention to your breath for two to five minutes, either by counting it or by letting your emotions get settled into the spaciousness and tranquility of your awareness and breath.

7: Think back

After completing the practice, think back on it. What bodily sensations did you experience? Did they become better or different after you explored them? Was it simple to be compassionate toward your anger? If so, how did you achieve it? Did your anger then lessen?

Write down your responses to these questions in your journal and consider them. This will reassure you that you are capable of controlling your anger as well as any other emotions.

Additionally, this shifts your viewpoint on anger and encourages you to accept it patiently and without passing judgment. These two mindsets support the development and reinforcement of mindfulness.

As you make progress, go through the preceding procedures and techniques at least once a day and whenever you catch yourself getting upset or angry. You will eventually become skilled at it and will find it effortless to let go of anger whenever it arises.

"Vengeful anger" refers to an intense and almost obsessive fascination with the person you believe has wronged you, often accompanied by thoughts of exacting revenge. Dr. Chris Aiken, M.D. warns that this kind of anger can be physically, emotionally, and mentally draining, leading to stress and a variety of health issues. "Studies reveal that when someone wrongs you, and you have the chance to exact revenge, the brain's dopamine or reward center becomes activated in a way that is similar to addictions." Put another way, the pleasant and addictive nature of retribution accounts for the propensity of enraged individuals to obsess over concepts of vengeance that grow increasingly intense in their minds."

Vengeful rage can be partly defeated by finding something else to occupy your time. "A good approach for this type of anger is to find activities that get you out of your head, such as volunteering, which shifts your brain from anger at others toward helping others," advises Dr. Aiken.

For the APA, Michael Price writes, "Who's right? Psychologists are studying the brain processes that underlie retaliation and discovering that, depending on the situation and the person, both may be. Retaliation might remind others that you're a serious person if you're a power-seeker. In societies with lax legal enforcement, retaliation serves as a means of maintaining order. But there is a cost to retaliation. According to psychologists' studies, it can make you stay dissatisfied and concentrate on the circumstance rather than allowing you to continue your life. Humans are terrible at anticipating the implications of retribution, even though it is a human reaction to being wrong."

PETRIFIED fury: Also called hardened fury, this kind of rage arises when you grow resentful of someone or something and find it difficult to let go, forget, and go on. Dr. Peter Sacco says that petrified anger results from someone holding onto a sense of bitterness and hatred. Although you're waiting for an apology, the offending party may be unaware of your anger. You have to acknowledge that your anger isn't helping you. You can forgive someone unconditionally, even if you're no longer in contact with them. In doing so, you'll also be able to forgive yourself."

You can eventually grow accustomed to harboring resentment and start to consider these emotions normal in your day-to-day life. However, the longer you hold on to the hurt, frustration, or disappointment caused by someone else, the more bitter you become and the harder you feel anger in your heart.

Incidental anger: This type of anger can result from an unforeseen event or circumstance and be appropriately expressed to the appropriate person involved, leading to immediate rectification. Occasionally, anger is characterized by a sudden outburst that is resolved immediately or prompts appropriate action once it is dealt with.

According to Houston, Texas-based Cynthia Pavlock of The Center for Anger Resolution, "Anger is not a bad or terrible emotion; rather, it helps us sense that something is wrong." It's okay to have an experience that makes you angry; just let it out and move on."

Empathic or sympathetic anger: This kind of anger can also be healthy if it motivates appropriate action or change. Empathic anger is directed toward another person, particularly someone who has been wronged or treated unfairly. Empathic anger can motivate you to act or launch a worthy cause on behalf of someone, mainly because of the justifiable outrage you felt for that person or cause.

Suppose a neighbor in your neighborhood has received unfair treatment, for example. In that case, you might become very upset on their behalf and create a petition asking your neighborhood to stand by the person or family and demand that justice be served or that appropriate measures be taken. According to Dr. Chris Aiken, mental health generally improves when we put others before ourselves, even though it is common knowledge that self-care and self-time should be scheduled. For instance, compared to performing the same task for compensation, people report higher enjoyment when they volunteer directly and face-to-face with others."

Calming down

Managing your anger can often be as easy as stepping back and counting to 10. There are many techniques and methods to quickly relieve yourself of anger so that you can live a life of love, happiness, and prosperity. Here are a few tools to help you control your anger more effectively. They help prevent you from going past the point of return.

Pets

Raising a pet can be amazing for anyone's life. The love, positivity, and warmth a pet radiates are priceless and cannot be found elsewhere. They will help you stay centered, and it is not a coincidence that pets are assigned to terminally ill people to increase their will to fight to live longer. Science shows that seniors who live with pets develop less age-related illnesses. Be careful choosing a pet whose previous owner may have been abused.

Learn how to laugh more. Learn to make more jokes and humor in situations. By laughing and smiling, endorphins, which are feel-good chemicals, are released into the body. Essentially, the more laughter one experiences, the better physically one will feel. It improves your health and relationships, slows aging, and increases longevity. In the heat of the moment, humor is an excellent weapon that can diffuse anger. It disarms both parties and releases the tension created in the atmosphere. It also stabilizes your blood pressure, calms your thoughts, and allows you to think more logically.

Music

Science shows plants grow towards positive, happy music, just as they levitate towards the sun. Take that in for a minute: how powerful could music be for your mind if plants react positively to music? Whenever you feel stressed, agitated, or angry, put on your favorite album and let it engulf you in calmness.

Prayer

The power of prayer has incredible power if you are in it. Nothing is more powerful than a prayer to calm your mind and state. Anger disrupts the soul, body, and mind. Asking the lord for strength will send surging energy through your soul to instantly relieve you of all stress.

The prayers ensure a layer of protection and shield for you and keep you grounded. Understand and remember that anger is simply your perception of what is unfair or threatening to you. However, if you are angry and know that God is watching you, you can instantly transform all negative energy into positive energy.

Friends

The greatest poverty in this life is knowing that no one cares about your well-being. There is absolutely nothing worse and lonelier than this empty feeling. Humans long for love and companionship; without them, we would feel isolated and lonely beyond despair.

Set dates aside for your friends and enjoy the time with all your attention. Identify at least one person to share your troubles and frustrations with. Talk with this friend as much as possible to voice your fears, frustrations, and anger.

By releasing this frustration with your friend, you realize that the issues and conflicts are of little significance sometimes. You will eventually feel better and gain more control of your anger.

ANXIETY, FEAR, AND ANGER

Anxiety in a panic disorder mixes intense terror with numerous other physical symptoms. A physical assault can occur anywhere at any time. This plays a significant role in the fear it causes the person experiencing such things. They are frequently taken aback by surprise when it occurs. Panic attacks can happen in broad daylight, at night in a dimly lit place, or while you're by yourself in bed. A moody collection of uncontrollable anxiety and fear combined with a condition of confusion or depression frequently indicates the appropriate diagnosis of a psychological disorder.

These symptoms can appear quickly; they frequently peak in ten minutes or less. Burning feelings, hot and cold flashes, tunnel vision, and vomiting may accompany these.

A person experiencing a panic attack may occasionally feel as though they are dying. Experiencing these things could make someone lash out at those around them in fear and rage. People respond differently to the same situation. People may occasionally react violently, while others may draw themselves in and wish for things to change. Everybody experiences it differently.

Numerous factors might contribute to an individual's pain, which can result in anxiety disorders. There could be a lot of tension from the job. One of these attacks is known to be initiated by the death of a loved one. Sometimes, it could be as simple as the fear of speaking in front of others. Additionally, heterogeneity may have contributed to this disorder. Additionally, there may be a connection between panic disorders and other conditions' symptoms. Situations such as sexual harassment or marital violence can result in psychological disorders.

Treatment for Parkinson's disease varies from one individual to the next. A doctor will frequently attempt to manage the condition with tranquilizers. Anyone experiencing these symptoms must seek medical attention from a qualified expert. Psychological counseling is required. Effective techniques like cognitive behavioral therapy can also greatly treat this sickness. Applying breathing and meditation techniques to address the symptoms can also be very beneficial.

Furthermore, the majority of illnesses stem from emotional or stressful conditions that we trigger from within. Naturally, this includes fear and worry, which are gradually covered in the preceding chapters. Our occupation and the people we know or live with only contribute to intensifying a particular sensation that we are susceptible to, which in turn activates our anxiety, worry, or terror. Anxiety and stress are forces that operate on your body, organs, or cells, leading to malfunction and degradation. Streptococcus pneumoniae produces pus that stays in your cells and in the lymph fluid that surrounds your cells.

An allergic reaction to bodily toxins like cancer. Cancer grows in an aging body because germs live and multiply in an aging body. Accid destroys cell structures and tissue.

Your diet might either contribute to an unhealthy or alkaline body. Your body produces acid from processed food. Eating raw food lowers the acidity in your body and returns it to a normal state.

The Nature of Fear

What is a fair?

The majority of us do not want to experience fear. Conjuring up images of being completely overwhelmed and debilitated can make the body react to the concept of a faint with pressure in the chest, sick feelings in the stomach, and even a rapid heartbeat. Thus, it is understandable that we do not desire to feel fear.

By being willing to meet often, face to face, you allow yourself to feel the fear and let it dissolve before you, revealing that it is nothing when fully encountered! The greatest fear was the fear of the fear.

Fear is the opposite of anger. Some claim that fury breeds rage. People exhibit varying degrees of fear aversion. This means that to control your anger, you must control your fear. The most profound, most powerful, and most complex emotion is fear. We are all affected by "Fear" differently depending on our childhood experiences or education. In most cultures, being afraid is virtually sinful. Every parent dislikes seeing their kids act fearfully. Thus, parents teach their children not to be afraid. Be courageous. Don't cry. Avoid being afraid.

Therefore, the most controlled intended emotion is fear. Most people learn by age

10 or 11 how to hide their fear even from themselves. Many feel influenced if their body tells them they are afraid. Ask your child whether they are afraid, and they will likely say "No" while putting on an irate expression and asking why you asked. However, the reality of life is that everyone experiences grief. Due to its complex and mixed nature, fear is a unique emotion affecting us all. It might be easier if someone can openly and freely express their fear. Imagine that we don't need to conceal our fear. We don't need to cover it up with anger or other feelings.

Let Go of the Toxic Energy & Anger

I believe that all depressed people have some form of suppressed fury that governs all of their emotions. Because I'm so fascinated with human behavior, I've drawn many conclusions about what it takes for someone to be free. Because I have experienced the brink of destruction before and understand how helpless you feel in those circumstances, I have strong ideas regarding this subject and depression. I know the harm, confusion, and unworthiness you do to yourself every day.

Despite their obvious rage, I've encountered individuals who tell me they're not angry people and never get upset. Not many people realize that anger may be a useful feeling. Everyone needs to experience anger occasionally because, without it, one would become numb and a people-pleaser. The frightening thing is that every single person I have treated with has suppressed rage of some type. It was all unconscious; they were unaware of it. I was among those individuals. When I was in my early 20s, I used to work out. I didn't even realize why I felt so miserable because I was suppressing so much rage. Even though I was making progress, I could still feel it, and until I figured out how to let go of it, it crippled everything I did.

Experiencing tremendous rage is the best way to let it out. I've repressed my anger by doing this over the years when I felt like getting furious. I walk into a room or a car and simply let everything out when alone. I consider what irritates me, and I continue piling on things until the angry mood begins to overpower me. I'm heating up in this condition, and because it's a release, adrenaline pours through my body, and I feel alive again.

Feelings of strain or tension govern all you do in life. When we need to use the restroom, we apply pressure to release our stress. Our bodies tense up during a romantic encounter, and we want to let go. I feel compelled to tell you the truth even though I realize this goes against what the typical person would say. Anger is precisely the same. I think it's healthy to let out your anger and get it off your chest, so I don't think utilizing medicines to control rage is a good idea.

I'm not saying you have to utilize this every time; I'm just offering you some viable alternatives that, if you take, will significantly alter your behavior and emotions of depression.

You feel liberated when you let go of anything in life. Freedom arises from releasing the energy that most people have shackled themselves with so that it can no longer govern them. You know those moments when you lose your cool with a family member, and it feels like you have no control at all? That is the result of not releasing yourself from that negative energy regularly. I used to try to make everyone I came into contact with happy when I was younger. All I wanted was for people to accept and like me, yet this came at a cost.

Most of the time, I would just suck up to these individuals, and they would just laugh and make fun of me because all I wanted was for them to like me. During my time in school, I used to cope frequently, but I had no idea how to improve my situation. I understood deep down that it was because I didn't own who I was; thus, it would make me feel furious and unhappy. The anger would also grow. If I were being authentic, I wouldn't put up with that behavior from others, but instead, I would laugh at their criticism of me. Throughout school, a lot of your values and views are formed.

For instance, you will believe it everywhere you go if you are extremely attractive and others have told you so your entire life. You will also receive praise regularly. The handsome person will have far less limiting beliefs than the person who has been termed unattractive and a loser throughout school. It's as though you were adored without conditions from the moment of your birth till you grew older. You went to new places and met new people. You start expecting that love from everyone when you step outside the unconditional love paradigm, and you frequently lose it.

As we grow, we are like sponges, and every new experience impacts our lives for better or worse. A person with a bad upbringing will give a lot of reasons for why they are unable to overcome their depression and claim that it is entirely their fault. Despite being what is known as a "hard case," they are nonetheless able to achieve their goals in life. All you need to know is that getting out of your rut will be more difficult. Although it's difficult to translate now, you can use it to your advantage. I wouldn't have been able to absorb or understand anything if this had been explained while I was stuck. It all comes down to taking each day as it comes and genuinely committing to improving yourself every day. Notable figures such as Martin Luther King, Gandhi, and John F. Kennedy experienced severe depression and thought it would never end. However, they realized that they were the only ones harming themselves, and everything changed for them as they began to work and develop a sense of self-worth.

When you're depressed and angry, you start thinking about death negatively and ask yourself, "If only I died, the pain would stop." In actuality, depression makes it difficult to recall good thoughts and makes you believe that you never will. I used to tell myself that since I wouldn't have much time left, I may as well enjoy life to the fullest. Although it's simple to say and much more difficult to perform, I was compelled to change when I gave it my full attention.

www.ingramcontent.com/pod-product-compliance
Lightning Source LLC
Chambersburg PA
CBHW052135110526
44591CB00012B/1728